dejlige days

dejlige days

MY GUIDE TO A SUCCESSFUL RELOCATION

by melanie haynes

contents

INTRODUCTION

my relocation story

Back in 2008 we decided to move to another European country and, without ever visiting, I agreed to move to Copenhagen. The company my husband worked for had been offering him opportunities to work abroad for a long time and I had always been resistant as I wanted to work on my career. After a succession of soul-destroying months in my job as the company faced reduced budgets, redundancies and an uncertain future, I decided that it was time we took the chance on a new life. I have shared more about this relocation experience in Chapter Two.

We looked at our move as an adventure; if it didn't work out we could come back. After three months we were smitten, a year later my son was born and we continued to enjoy our Danish life.

We were lucky that when we moved we had the help of a fantastic relocation company which did a lot more than just find us a home but helped us with daily practical matters too. The transition into life here seemed easy and in truth I hadn't felt so excited about new experiences since I started university at eighteen.

By 2011 the impacts of the financial crisis were being felt and my husband was made redundant. We made the tough choice to move to Berlin where he was offered a job, and after our first relocation experience I tried to keep an open and positive mind, thinking, "How bad can it be?"

Three months after our move we had only just found a permanent place to live following a stint in a depressing and soulless corporate housing building. I was struggling physically and emotionally and just about holding it together for my then two year old son. Without support from a relocation company beyond the desperate search for our apartment, I was at sea with little to no German language skills – even the simplest of tasks felt impossible. I had been exploring the nearby neighbourhoods and found an English music class and started to find places to go with my son. I decided to write about these places on a blog – partly for my own sanity and also with the thought that if I could help one new expat mum feel less like I had at the start then it was worth it. I began to get emails from other mums thanking me for what I was doing. I was no longer living in a void and felt I had purpose. I have written a very honest and raw account of our experience in Berlin in Chapter Nine.

We were lucky enough to be able to return to Copenhagen in 2013 and resume our life here but I realised that, although I love this city, there are many women for whom Copenhagen is like Berlin was for me. I started a blog, Dejlige Days, for expats where I share recommendations, advice on settling in and the little idiosyncrasies of living here. I started getting emails asking for advice and also saw on many expat forums the need for support.

I saw that new expats needed help with the everyday things like getting to know their local area, shopping in a new country and transport systems. I conducted a survey and found that one of the biggest issues cited was overcoming feelings of isolation. Something I recalled very vividly from my time in Berlin.

So I decided to set up at a consultancy service helping to bridge the gap between the first stages of relocation and the real settling in period, the time when it feels the hardest to find your feet.

I wanted to add to this with more practical information and support, and this is what this book is all about.

WHY DID I WRITE THIS BOOK?

I have been writing this book for many years, both on paper and in my mind. Although I have embraced life in Copenhagen, I also really struggled with the move to Berlin. I thought about all the things that I learnt from tenaciously seeking out information to make life easier in an unknown place, how much of that information is in my head and how that could be shared with others making the first step into expat life. I also love helping people where I can.

I loved finding things out, having new experiences and changing my whole life when I moved to Copenhagen back in 2008. I was curious and brave and I learnt a lot about life in a different country, and a great deal about myself and the kind of life I wanted.

I approached my relocation to Berlin in the same way as the one to Copenhagen but found the adjustment different and wished I had more idea of how to tackle a new place that wasn't as open and friendly as I found Copenhagen. But it taught me a lot about how a relocation can be when it isn't easy, and how I wished I'd had someone to help me with their own experiences that would have made things just that little bit easier. I learnt to be a little bit tougher, a little bit braver and a lot more thick-skinned. It taught me what is important to me and my family.

In each chapter of this book I share the things that I have learnt from our three relocations in the last eight years. Some are things I enjoyed experiencing and others were things that I didn't, but going through them helped me learn about living in a different place and how to handle it.

I often share my experiences with new friends, other expats and clients through my relocation consultancy but there is so much I have in my head that can help others. My goal is to help people feel less daunted and less isolated by relocation and to have the chance to embrace the adventure. This book is me sharing my experiences in the hope of making other people's experience better.

WHO IS THIS BOOK FOR?

This book is like a friend sharing their experiences with you. Some chapters are longer than others but all have some real takeaway ideas on how to make many aspects of moving to, and living in, a new country easier. Whilst many relish the chance to find things out for themselves over time (like I did in the start), others have less time or energy, or more commitments and want to hit the ground running as I did in Berlin.

Other things are those you may not even realise that you need to know until they happen – dealing with a relocation consultant is something that few people will have done before, moving your children to a new home in a new country is a real challenge and there are many more aspects to relocation that I cover here. You can take or leave what you want from this book but everything I share here I believe would have helped me when I was a new expat. Many things I learnt the hard way and this can save you from that tough learning curve.

I have written this book from the me who moved to Copenhagen in 2008 child-free and ready for adventure and from the me who moved to Berlin and hit every expat challenge going. I have written it for the you who is daunted by relocation, the you who is excited but overwhelmed, the you who is scared and reluctant and the you who wants to be happy in a new country with a new life.

preparing to relocate – what you can do to make the move easier

Whether you have made an active choice to move to another country or it is a work necessity, there are still a lot of things you can do to help the process before you even start looking at places to live. It depends on how much time you have before your move as to how much you can do. Here are some of the basics I would recommend:

GET READING

Books are the perfect way to start. Choosing a few guide books about your new city can help familiarise yourself with the areas and the culture. A great start is to get the DK Eyewitness Top Ten Travel Guide for your city and the Lonely Planet guide. The first gives you a quick snapshot of the main tourist and cultural aspects. The second goes into much more and honest detail about the city and specific neighbourhoods, plus it looks at more social aspects so you can gain an understanding of the local culture.

Depending how popular your new location is for expats you may find there are some non-fiction memoirs about moving and living there. These are likely to be entertaining and informative at the same time, however do take them with a pinch of salt as there is likely to be an element of fictionalisation.

GET ONLINE (BUT TAKE IT EASY)

The Internet has a wealth of information but you can easily get bogged down in the sheer volume of information available. Start looking at basic level websites, for example the main tourist board website, websites from official bodies about moving to the city and search for any blogs written about moving to or living there. Bloggers will welcome and encourage interaction with their readers so they can be a big help. This shouldn't overwhelm you with too much information to start with. Once you feel you have an idea of the place you can read more widely but too much too soon can muddle you if you have no real terms of reference about the place. If a lot of the websites are in the local language use Google Chrome to get them translated, the translations are generally good.

TAKE A TRIP

If you have the time and finances, it is a great idea to take a trip to the new city for a long weekend and operate like a tourist with an agenda. Visit a few supermarkets to see what kind of food they sell and what the prices are like, and try to soak up some of the local culture. If you have time take a walk around the neighbourhoods you think you might like to live in and get a first impression. Relax but observe how people are and the atmosphere in the city – try and imagine yourself living there and ask yourself how that makes you feel.

A POSITIVE MINDSET FROM THE START

Start thinking of the move as an adventure even if you are reluctant or apprehensive about it. A positive attitude at the start can really be an asset, especially if you face setbacks or stressful situations associated with the move or at the start of your time there.

GET TALKING

Most likely you will have basic or no knowledge of the local language. If you can already speak the language you are well on the way to integrating quickly. Before both our moves to Denmark and Germany I learnt some basic language by using a book and CD in the first instance (it was 2007!) and later online resources. BBC Active Languages and Duolingo is a great start and, if it is available for the language you want to learn and you are prepared to make the financial investment, Rosetta Stone is excellent. I used this when we moved to Germany and it gave me a great introduction to the language. You will no doubt need further lessons when you get there but a very basic level of day-to-day words and phrases can really help you to feel less isolated in everyday life.

LOOK FOR SUPPORT FROM THE START

If you are moving to a position with a big company look at what they are offering in the way of support, especially if you are the spouse. In Denmark a lot of larger companies and organisations offer spouse mentoring schemes or newcomers groups. If this is available try and get some contacts early on so you have a seasoned expat to fire questions at but who also understands how you may be feeling. They will also remember how they felt or what was a mystery to them when they first moved so are a valuable resource. There are also forums you can join, for example Meetup groups or Facebook forums, where you can virtually meet people before you move. I found contacts I met via a Meetup group extremely helpful when I first moved to Berlin.

LOCAL ENGLISH LANGUAGE RESOURCES

Even if you want to live life like a local, finding out if there is an English language newspaper or news website can help in the transition. You can read about current affairs and issues in your new city. The adverts in these publications will be directly aimed at you and you are very likely to find information about language classes, integration meetings and courses you can take. I still enjoy reading English language news even though I am perfectly capable of reading Danish.

CHAPTER 2

my relocation story – copenhagen

Back in 2007 my husband and I got married after twelve years together (clearly we didn't rush into it!) and it felt like a new life was starting. I had been working for a not-for-profit organisation as Head of Communications for a few years. Over that time I had started to take control of my personal life (I lost two stone in weight, learnt to swim and got married) but my professional life was stressing me out. I had lost team members who were not being replaced due to budget cuts, office politics were reaching ridiculous levels and I was often in tears in the evening and waking at 5am unable to get back to sleep as I worried about the day ahead. This was no way to live.

For a number of years my husband's employers had been tempting him with exciting jobs abroad but I had always been reluctant – I was building my career. But suddenly that just seemed to not matter. I was working hard but getting very little back and I could see no real change on the horizon unless we made the change. So we did. It was late summer when he asked at work about possible places we could relocate to and was given the options of San Diego (too far from family), Germany (no – how ironic) and Copenhagen. So we settled on Copenhagen without me ever having visited. I bought some guide books and the process at my husband's work started.

I joined him just before Christmas whilst he was in Copenhagen for a week sorting out his new role. It was the first time I visited the city and I fell in love immediately: big beers, delicious real Danish pastries and sparkling Christmas lights. Apart from the superficial things I also liked the kind of lifestyle I saw around me and, chatting to various people we met along the way, it seemed to make people happy.

Once it was a sure thing, I spoke to my boss and arranged to leave my job at the end of the year (as it turned out they were generous enough to let me work almost until I left the country, extending my notice period on a monthly basis).

I finished work at the end of February 2008, having negotiated a year-long freelance contract to start in the summer so I would have some money coming in when we moved.

At the start of March we headed out to Copenhagen for our home search. We were met at our hotel by our relocation consultant, Caspar, who had a bag packed full of information about the city and life here. We viewed seven places in one day, a luxury that is no longer possible with the tough market now, and we had to give him a top three by the end of the day. It is funny that our initial number one was soon relegated to number three. I hadn't yet adjusted my expectations and had felt the modern apartment was the right one for us despite it being totally wrong. My husband gently talked me round to a beautiful late 19th century first floor apartment in Frederiksberg, which was of course perfect for us when we moved in.

Things moved quickly from that day – they accepted our offer and the moving date of the 31st of March was set. We then had to get rid of about a third of our belongings, which we sold at a boot sale and a garage sale, and put more things in storage. In hindsight I wish I had been more brutal about getting rid of things but at this point we were not sure if our Copenhagen adventure would work out. We then put our house up for rental and arranged for packers to come in and pack up the remains of our belongings.

I am something of a control freak so you can imagine how I felt when I was bedridden (on the futon in the chaos of packing) with very bad tonsillitis. In fact the packing was all done efficiently without my interference. I was sad to be sick as I missed seeing my oldest friend and her newborn baby before we left.

All of a sudden we were at the new terminal 5 at Heathrow, with a suitcase and carry-on ready to start our new adventure.

At the time I was sharing my new life on a personal blog and this is what I wrote about that first day:

Handover today went well, the flat is much bigger than I remembered so everything went in fine. The removal men turned up with the truck at about 11.30am and were unpacked by 2pm even with unscheduled stops whilst our elderly new neighbour travelled down the stairs. If she was a better time manager she could have done all her errands in one go but at least it keeps her fit!

I visited our local Irma (a supermarket chain similar to Waitrose) several times in the day and made friends with the young manager, Peter, who was happy to help with my queries about the many types of cream they sold. He also welcomed me to the neighbourhood.

After we unpacked random boxes and the kitchen we went for a quest to find a DIY shop which took us miles only to buy the plugs in a supermarket having given up on the directions we had. On the walk back, about 2 yards from the supermarket, we spotted the shop. Sadly my current vocab doesn't extend to DIY!

The area seems really nice with plenty of shops, bars and restaurants on Gammel Kongevej, the only street we have explored so far. It is very quiet in our apartment even though we back onto a school, they seem to do lessons in shifts as there always seems to be a teeming playground. Bizarrely the school bell rang at quarter to ten tonight. We can't hear neighbours so I am hoping that they can't hear us!

Other bizarre observation of the day – they leave babies outside shops and cafes unattended as 'the fresh air is good for them'!

From that first day onwards I felt a fizz of excitement in my tummy every morning. After a few mornings with our relocator, we were registered with resident numbers and he had taken us around our local big supermarkets, which at the time I thought was a strange excursion but it was a great thing to do to help me get acclimatised.

I decided to take a month before I started Danish lessons and took that time to explore the local area and dig into the city. We spent weekends exploring places such as Christiania (which I loved but my husband hated) and many of the touristy places. In those days there was no social media to guide us so we explored blind, and it was amazing. I felt like an explorer; every day I found new places, had new experiences and excitedly shared these with my husband every evening.

One afternoon in our local supermarket I heard a very clear English voice and I bravely walked up to a very statuesque woman and introduced myself. This was my first friend. Selim had also just moved to Copenhagen from the US (although she was from Ghana and had been at boarding school in the UK, hence the accent). We met for coffee later in the week and I noticed she carried a little leather bound notebook into which she wrote down recommendations and information she discovered. I liked this and her. We parted without making another date and I wasn't sure we would meet again.

Fast forward a few weeks and guess who was in my first Danish class? We became good friends and even ended up having our sons within weeks of each other a few years later. I was glad I made the bold step of speaking to her in the supermarket.

I think I spent a lot of that first year in a constant state of excitement. I balanced my days with Danish lessons in the morning, some freelance work in the afternoons and a lot of exploring, often on a whim. I met people in class and soon realised which people I had more in common with, I got to know my neighbours and I found a feeling of peace that had been lacking for a long time in the UK. One May evening we sat eating our dinner with the windows open, birds singing outside and I turned to my husband and said how much I loved our new life, and he agreed.

I look back and wonder what made the experience so good. I think it was a combination of many things. The disillusionment with my life in the UK meant that I was open to a new experience. My parents had already moved from the UK to France so I didn't feel I was leaving anyone behind (friends were more than happy to plan trips to visit). Our move was actually very stress-free, from the home search through to the actual move, and then the subsequent settling in period (a lot of which was helped by a brilliant relocator). I found that the Danish way of life suited me – being car-free was brilliant. Moving in the summer so the days were long and we had great weather meant that we could explore a lot more. We did tons more things in the evenings than we ever did at home without the long car commute at the end of the day. We saw things were happening and we went along. We went to watch dragon boats racing at Island Brygge – it turned out to be a company team building event but we sat in the sunshine at 9pm and just enjoyed ourselves with no pressure. We went along to a free concert to hear Tina Dickow. We lived a lot more spontaneously than we ever did in the UK. We had more time together and life was more relaxed in general.

After our first calendar year in Copenhagen we decided to start a family and we were lucky enough that I fell pregnant quickly (I always wonder how quickly this would have been if I had still been run ragged in the UK). A whole new journey started.

CHAPTER 3

sharing the news of your move with loved ones

Once you have started thinking about moving it is then time to share this with some friends and family. Usually at the beginning people share the news with some close friends and family so they can have help and support, but others choose to keep it private until the decision is made.

Either way there are a few standard responses you can expect. The most important thing to remember if you receive a reaction you don't like is that it is about the person, not you or your decision. At the same time you need to be understanding about how others will feel at this time – grandparents may fear losing touch with their grandchildren, friends will feel they are losing you. There are ways you can deal with these reactions, which vary from kindness to dismissal at either end of the spectrum.

THE POSITIVES

"You are really brave!"

When people say this to you, they are not trying to worry you. In most cases they really think it and many feel they couldn't ever contemplate making such a huge move. They admire what you are doing and usually this statement is a person being supportive.

It can, however, cause you to start to panic a little, especially if you didn't think what you are doing is particularly brave and then start to think that you need bravery to continue. I think it is fair to say that it is brave to pack up your life, even for a set period of time, and transport yourself to a whole new place and culture. When you encounter this reaction, take it as a compliment and let it embolden you. As they say, being brave is being scared but doing it anyway!

"I wish I could do that."

Envy from people, especially friends, will happen as many people feel trapped in their lives and would love to try something new, even if they aren't able to do it. These are the people who will be the most interested in your plans and new life, and you may even inspire them to make changes to their lives.

"How exciting!"

This is the response you most want to hear and I hope it is the one you hear the most as it *is* exciting, and you want a big cheering squad behind you as you embark on this new stage of life.

THE NEGATIVES

"You are judging how we live."

This is often a negative reaction you will encounter. Seeing someone doing something different to you can seem like a criticism of how you are doing things. When I talk about how great I find living a car-free life, car owning friends in the UK can get defensive and say how they couldn't be car-free for a multitude of reasons. My choice is not a slight on others, it works for me and my circumstances but maybe not for them. People's own resentments of their lives, even if they don't realise it, will surface when they see others making a change or doing something fundamentally different. This is a key example of

'It's about them and not you'. Try and let this one wash over you and perhaps, depending on how much it bothers you to offend this person, play down the positive attributes of your potential new life. You may also decide not to share too much about your plans.

"I don't understand, why would you want to move so far away,
we'll never see you."

Guilt is one of the big emotions you will encounter. It is natural to already have a small feeling of guilt about what you are doing, but this can be heightened by being made to feel even more guilty by those very close to you.

They may not want or intend to make you feel guilty but it is something you need to deal with. It is tough to have loved ones move a long way from you. I dealt, not very well, with this when my parents moved to France when I was in my twenties. But there are practical ways you can deal with this. Firstly, it is important to tell your loved ones that you are not finding leaving them easy, that you will miss them, even though you are positive and excited about the step you are making.

Make plans for when they can visit you even before you have moved. A big part of this reaction from loved ones is motivated by worry for you and the fact that they won't be near to help and support you. Unless where you are moving is the other side of the globe, cheap airfares will mean you can still see your family easily and you may be surprised how much they actually enjoy visiting you in your new city. This is one of the reactions you need to deal with sensitively, even if it causes you resentment. It is always harder to be the one left behind than the one having the adventure.

INDIFFERENCE

This was a curious and quite common one I encountered, but it was generally from people I wasn't that close to. As a person I have always been very curious about other cultures and ways of doing things and I was surprised that more people were not fascinated by our plans to leave the UK to move to Denmark and later to Berlin. But I guess other people have their own lives to think about!

WAYS TO TELL PEOPLE AND HOW TO DEAL WITH IT

You will know your friends and family best but the general rule of thumb is to share the news with those closest to you first and early on in the process, and be prepared to encounter both negativity and positivity. Also, remember the initial reaction will be driven by shock, in most cases, so don't take the first things people say or do too much to heart. Let them mull it over, talk about it without you and then discuss it again. The reaction then will most probably be very different.

I wouldn't make a huge announcement in a big public way – tailor each one to the people you are telling. Think in advance how you think people will react and have your responses ready. You may need to reassure or celebrate but you need to be ready.

You also need to be ready to deal with how people's reactions will make you feel. It is common to feel an element of doubt about what you are doing in the face of negativity, and you will feel you want to have some reassurance that what you are doing is OK. It's a good idea to identify the most positive person in your circle, who may not be the closest person to you, to tell first in confidence about your plans. But the most important thing is not to let any reactions put you off your plans, if you have thought them through and you (and your partner and family) are happy about it then that is the most important thing – after all it is you that is taking the leap.

CHAPTER 4

managing a relocation consultant

Depending where you are relocating to and the level of the new job you may be fortunate enough to be offered the services of a relocation consultant, or at least decide to use your own.

There are enormous benefits to using a relocation service, especially when it comes to finding somewhere to live that suits you and your budget. Having the inside track on life in the new city, from the culture to the bureaucracy, is also really useful.

The relocation company will be chosen by the new employers hopefully because they have been successful in finding people suitable accommodation. They will also often handle registrations and opening bank accounts in your new country. However, not all relocation consultants are created equal and there are certainly a number of ways you can make sure you get the most out of their services.

BEING CLEAR FROM THE START

You need to be clear from the outset what your relocation consultant can do for you within the package offered by your new employers. There may be a

19

maximum number of properties they are permitted to show you, as was the case when we moved to Berlin, and if the market is tough you may get through your allocation pretty swiftly.

Find out from the start what is offered within the package and perhaps renegotiate the terms before the process starts. It may be the case that you will want to do some things yourself and keep the areas where their expertise lies in reserve.

THINK ABOUT YOUR BUDGET CAREFULLY

One of the first things they will ask is what is your budget for rent. For many people moving to a new country this is a total guess. Make sure you ask your consultant for honest advice on what you should expect to pay for your desired level of accommodation before you think about this figure. You should also consider other associated costs such as heating and TV which may be added to the base rent price but will need to be paid.

It is important that you set a reasonable budget, but it is also useful to set an absolute maximum as you may find that your first figure is not enough for what you need or what is available. You don't want to have to scramble about doing calculations. Tell your consultant the first figure but keep the other one in reserve.

TAKE THE INITIATIVE

To a certain extent you can't be totally reliant on your consultant. Use property rental websites to get an idea of the type of accommodation you are likely to be looking at, both in your budget and desired location. In our case when moving to Berlin our consultant gave us a login to the rental portal she used so we would browse ourselves and also make notes about places for her to see. Making notes about properties is essential as after some time looking you can forget which property was which and why you liked or didn't like one. Also, if you see a pattern emerging of reasons why you are rejecting places you need to make sure your consultant is aware of this.

THINK REALISTICALLY

I know this is something I will keep coming back to but realistic expectations are essential. This is another area your consultant should be able to help you with.

Before you start working with the consultant you need to do some clear thinking of your own about how you see your new life. Do you want real city living in a central apartment or a more suburban lifestyle in a house? We downsized from a four bedroom detached house in the UK to a 100square metre, four room (excluding kitchen and bathroom) city apartment, but we loved it. The space was perfect for us at that time. You need to think about how many rooms you really need. When we were just a couple we wanted a second room which could be used as a guest room for the few weeks of the year people visited, and it also doubled up as office space. But you need to think about how important that extra room is, and is it worth the extra money in rent.

SET YOUR PRIORITIES HONESTLY

Setting your priorities is important, but you need to be prepared to be flexible. We were advised to think of our top three priorities for our new place. Was location very important? Was the number of rooms and size of the apartment an issue? Do you need an elevator (a dream in some period apartment buildings in Northern Europe)? If so, and one isn't available, then what is the highest floor you are prepared to trek up to? Are you bringing a pet? Do you have a car? Parking can be an issue in some city areas. Do you need your own laundry room or washing machine, or are you happy to share a communal one (as is often the case in Copenhagen)? There are many things you may think are important, but what are the real deal-breakers? You need to be realistic but at the same time flexible, as what you normally expect from your home country may not be possible.

LOCATION, LOCATION, LOCATION

I truly believe that location is the most important thing that can make or break a new relocation. I really think you can make an average apartment work if you are living in a great location; it is harder to make a bad location work even if the apartment is perfect. Think about areas of your new city you think you might like to move to, and again order them in priority. Usually this is dependent on the location of your new workplace, especially if you want to keep commuting time to a minimum, but you may be prepared to compromise on this for your perfect location or to find somewhere that fits your budget. Research beforehand is helpful, but so is asking your consultant for an honest view, and perhaps arranging a time with her or alone to visit some second choice areas. You can explore the areas around your potential apartments to get a feel of the local community. Also, take a look at Google Maps and Street View. It might not be immediately obvious what is close to you and potentially disruptive or disturbing if you were living there – like a school or a late night bar.

COMMUNICATE

I cannot stress enough the importance of communication – both ways – with your consultant. You need to be sure that they understand your ideas so they can give you relevant advice. If you feel really strongly against a place they have shown you, tell them and explain why. It will save time in the long run as you will avoid seeing more of the same. If you are very new to a city, get advice from your consultant about the areas they recommend in light of your budget and priorities. Also ask them if your priorities are realistic. I realise that time is often a luxury when relocating, but there is a lot you can do virtually to help aid your decision and maximise the time you do have with your consultant.

YOU ARE THE BOSS

Remember they are working for you; be confident but open to advice. If you are really not happy with the service your designated consultant is offering you, ask if you can have another one. I know no one wants to offend anyone, but once they are off the scene you can then be stuck in a situation that is wrong for you in the long term.

GIVE FEEDBACK AT THE END

You will probably breathe a huge sigh of relief once the final box is unpacked in your new home, but it is very worthwhile to share your experience with the relocation company. I am a big believer in giving feedback – both good and bad. Once you have found your home and registered and your contract is over with the relocation consultant, make sure you give feedback about the service you received. If things worked well, tell them, and if others didn't, say this too. If there were things where you could have used help or more assistance, tell them this too. All of this will help the next people.

relocating with children

We relocated once as a couple and twice with a child, and the experiences couldn't have been more different. You can be much more blasé about where you are living and how you move when you don't have a child or children to consider.

As part of readjusting your expectations about how and where you live you need to consider how families exist in the new environment. We would love to have a garden for our son to play in, but we also want to be close to other amenities such as parks, swimming pools and museums without needing to be reliant on using a car. Living in a new city means you need to adapt how your family lives.

YOUR HOME

Think carefully about how much space you really need as family. We live in a 140 square metre, two bedroom apartment on the third floor with no elevator. For many families this amount of space would be considered unworkable and far too small for a family of three.

Add in the traipsing up the stairs many times a day with a child or baby and shopping. We chose to live in this space and it works for us for now, but for others it might not. We try and keep possessions and clutter under control – no mean feat with a six year old and a 40 something semi-hoarder, but we need to. Living in cities such as Copenhagen and Berlin often means living in an apartment, so you need to think how you are going to make this work for you. Perhaps you will only consider apartments on lower floors or on higher floors with an elevator (although in the current rental market in many major cities, you may not be in a position to be too picky).

You also need to think about practical things outside the home as well such as the availability of childcare (if you need it), playgrounds and open spaces within easy reach, shops selling things you need on a daily basis, proximity to public transport. The essentials in life need to be that much closer when you have young children – as a family you need to be clear about what the essentials are for your family. This will look different for everyone, but it is an important exercise to do honestly and with an element of flexibility.

PREPARING TO MOVE – PACKING AND STORAGE

Over the last few moves we have fine-tuned how we manage it with a preschool child. The first thing I would recommend if you can afford it (and I would always sacrifice something else for this) is to have experts come into your home and pack it up for you. They know what they are doing, they do it fast and thoroughly and if anything does get broken you are covered by their insurance (and I would strongly recommend that you take out the insurance). You can then escape the house with your child and feel a lot less stressed about it. When we left Berlin we had packers in for a 24-hour period and we stayed in a hotel for the night. This meant they could work on until it was finished.

Before the packers even arrive you need to be brutal and decide if everything you are taking is essential. Firstly, you will be charged by the space your belongings take up in the removal truck and the time it takes the packers to pack. As I mentioned previously, we moved from a four bedroom detached house in the UK to a 100 square metre apartment in Copenhagen. We simply couldn't take everything, nor did we really need it all. Think about your new life and what is really essential. I find it very cathartic clearing the junk out every time we move, and I think I am getting better at not keeping something 'just in case'. Perfect time for things you hate to 'go missing'! At the same time, with children you need to think about making sure they have continuity in their immediate surroundings.

If your move is temporary or you are unsure if you will stay longer term, you can consider taking a small storage unit in your home country to store the special things you don't want to move with you. But a word of caution: if you decide not to move back you need to deal with this stuff at some point. I recall going back to our storage unit and making very poor decisions as to what to throw out, and I wished I had been more thoughtful (and brutal) when I first stored it.

SHOW DON'T TELL

I find that you can speak to children about things but showing them works much better.

Look at pictures of your new city online together and talk about things you can do together in the new city. This is easier as these things will be there no matter where you live in the city. Home in on your child's interests, whether they are museums, parks or a specific hobby, and find place they will be able to do these things, then research them together.

If possible, look for books aimed at children about either moving to or visiting the new city

- both fiction and factual books are often available. If you are lucky enough to move to

Paris you will be spoilt for choice! My son loves books and sees things in them as 'official', and they carry more weight than me saying the same things. A quick Amazon search for these books is a great way to source them.

GETTING CHILDREN INVOLVED AND MANAGING EXPECTATIONS

Children can find moving stressful, and a lot of this comes from the stress they sense from their parents. Suddenly there is massive change around them, familiar things are being packed up and everything is different. I found that I needed to make sure my son understood things that were happening around him. Even when he was two we explained what was happening in an appropriate way. However, I wouldn't talk in any concrete terms about a new home until you know it's yours as children often become fixated on a tiny detail, and if it isn't there they can get very upset.

We made it into an adventure. With our first move my son and I went stay with my parents in France whilst the apartment was packed up and my husband got us settled in temporary housing in Berlin. For a little child this was the perfect buffer between places.

As he got older we involved him as much as we could. Giving him responsibility for packing his precious Lego creations meant that he wasn't worrying and fixating on them getting damaged. Make sure your packers label things clearly so you can find the boxes you need quickly at the other end. Before we made our last move we read a book about a little girl who was moving house with her family. Her mum gave her a pack of big colourful stickers to put on the boxes of her things so she knew which were hers. We did this and it worked on so many levels – our son felt in control of his things and it kept him occupied.

We showed him the places we were looking at online, and when we went to look around we made sure he felt involved and that he felt he had an opinion that was listened to.

Ultimately the decision is ours but we do all have to live there.

The key at this stage is involvement and listening to your child. You may feel you have a million things to think about, but investment in your child at this time helps with the long term settling in. Moving country will have an impact on your child, even in a tiny way, and you need to be kind to yourself and them during this period.

DURING THE MOVE AND THE EARLY DAYS

Once you have moved in, when it is possible remove your child from the situation as much as possible. Unpacking is messy and chaotic even with the most well organised families. As I am something of a control freak, we find the best way is for my husband to take my son out and about for a fun day (or three) whilst I tackle the box mountains.

Before you do much else I would unpack, with your child, their stuff and decide how it should be organised in their new room. Familiar things around will make your child calmer and also means they have stuff to be playing with whilst you sort out other matters.

We all like to feed our children good things but it's not the end of the world if they get a few takeaways or easy meals during this time – it all adds to the adventure. But try and keep to normal schedules as much as possible – adding more upheaval to a period of change is never a good idea. Sometimes the impact of the move will occur later once the dust settles. Keeping it all as stress-free as possible can help with this, but remember your child may take longer to process the move and its implications than you think. Our son definitely seemed to struggle more with moving in the months after the move than at the time as he gradually realised familiar things were different.

To be honest, we all want our children to be happy but most of this advice is aimed at keeping parents sane! Try to take some time out from unpacking for family time – the aforementioned pizza, an exploration of your new neighbourhood, a visit to a new playground, just some breathing space.

CHAPTER 6

temporary housing

Sometimes it is not possible to move straight into your own home and many people choose the convenient option of serviced temporary housing or renting an Airbnb whilst they search for an apartment. Actually living in the place in which you are searching for a home gives you a significant advantage, but it doesn't come without complications.

CHOOSING YOUR TEMPORARY HOME

We stayed in serviced corporate apartments, which serve a purpose but are not particularly cosy. Most cities have these kinds of places available for short or mid term rentals. A benefit of corporate apartments is that you can keep the rental rolling over if your home search is taking longer than you anticipated. Usually there is a point in the month where you need to arrange the next month's rental. The downside of these places is the feeling of being unsettled and not quite living in the city yet.

The other option is Airbnb and this offers a more home-from-home experience. This is an option I would favour if I were moving again, but of course there is less flexibility in extending your stay and the rentals may be shorter term. Katie and her husband, who we will hear from in Chapter Twelve, took this route and they found it gave them breathing space to settle into Copenhagen and find the right long term rental for them, but with a feeling of actually living in the city from the start.

THE BENEFITS

The biggest benefit of taking a temporary rental is you are already on the ground and able to view apartments more easily than if you are only travelling for short home search visits. In a fast moving rental market you will often need to arrange to see an apartment within a short time to avoid missing out on it.

It also means you can start to get settled and explore the city, especially if you are unsure about where exactly in your new city you wish to live. I spent a lot of time in Berlin visiting different areas to see if they appealed to us. I would advise, if possible, taking temporary housing close to at least one of your preferred neighbourhoods so you don't end up spending too much time travelling unnecessarily, and where you can easily experience the local area and community.

Another big benefit is that the apartment has the basics you need and will, for a cost, be cleaned for you, with bedding and towels provided. We lived for almost four months in temporary housing in Berlin and there were certainly benefits to this.

THE DOWNSIDE

It can be stressful with no set time limit to living in a temporary home, especially if you don't like the area around your place or it just starts to feel soulless and you yearn for your own space and things.

WHAT CAN YOU DO TO MAKE IT A POSITIVE EXPERIENCE?

We learned a lot from living in corporate housing and there were a few things we did, or could have done in hindsight, to make the experience better:

TECHNOLOGY

Something of a no-brainer but make sure you have a laptop or tablet to connect to the Internet as this is essential for entertainment, research and keeping up with people at home, especially as you may not be able to get a phone contract easily at the start. However, the Internet access may not be great if you are living in a large complex – we had to sit in the kitchen pressed up against the wall in our place to get any decent connection!

RESEARCH

Before you move in do a lot of research about the area around your housing as this will help you feel less isolated. Understanding the transport links from your area to other parts of the city is also important. If you have a choice of locations make sure you check you are happy with the one you chose, especially if this is part of your relocation consultancy as they may be pressuring you to choose the one *they* think is best but that may not be for you. We ended up in a place too far from the areas we were looking at apartments to rent in and it was in a less than salubrious area, not great when I was usually on my own with a two year old.

BRING YOUR ESSENTIALS

Although the places will be furnished and equipped you still should pack a box of essentials from home before you pack up and move to the temporary housing, and have it sent to arrive when you do. We moved in the autumn to Berlin and hoped to be settled quickly but this didn't happen so I was pleased I had shipped a box of our winter essentials. Other things to consider sending in a box are: favourite toys and books (if you have children) and a change of season clothes if you are moving towards the end of a season.

The kitchen in our place had a very basic selection of utensils. I bought some cheap things from the supermarket such as a cheese grater and measuring jug. So be prepared, if you like cooking perhaps add some of your kitchen essentials and basic cooking utensils like a measuring jug, measuring spoons (basically anything that measures!), a cheese grater and a tin opener to your box you send from home.

CAPSULE WARDROBES

As you will probably be travelling quite light at this stage, be prepared to be sick of the small selection of clothes you bring by the end of the stay. Don't bring anything you love too much. There were washing facilities in the block we stayed in and they needed tokens, which could be bought from the management office on certain days of the week. As the machines are used by lots of people, they are not the most efficient in the world. Unless you want to buy a drying rack, make sure all the clothes you bring are dryer friendly.

KEEP POSITIVE

Living in temporary housing and searching for a home can start to become emotionally draining. It can feel like a never-ending jail term if your home search is longer than you hoped, but the main thing to keep in mind is that this is temporary – this is not your ultimate home and you will have your own things again.

CHAPTER 7

adjusting your expectations

Changing your life by moving to a new country and a new city can be made easier by being open to adjusting your expectations of how your life should be.

YOUR HOME

When we first moved to Denmark I was still in the mindset that a newer build home was better than a period one. We had lived for most of our post-university life in new or newish build places, and when I was given the choice between a well proportioned hundred year old apartment and one that was not so well suited to us but was new, my newly expat brain initially plumped for the latter. Luckily my husband had a little more forethought about our new life and we went with the former. It was perfect for us.

What you can expect from housing varies from country to country and from city to city. It also depends if you are downsizing in your move. We moved into about half the space we had in the UK and we often hear friends in the UK saying they need more space to live in, but it is important to actually think about the space you will need to live in to be happy.

If you need a bigger space for children, pets or your specific lifestyle, then you need to think about this at the start of your home search. However, you may find that the expectations you had in your home country will change, as mine did.

DAILY LIFE

Without doubt your daily life will be completely different once you move. For example, at home you may have both been working and in the new country only one person may have a job in the early stages. As the person not working you will find that you have long days to fill, and if you have children you may find that you are spending a lot more time with them than before. This can be a struggle and adjustment for all parties. As the person working you may be faced with a frustrated partner on your return home in the evening. There is a big reason why many big companies offer spouse support as one of the most common reasons that expat workers return home is that their partner is not happy.

Whilst the change can be challenging you can see it as a gift of time to be able to explore your new city, and also to explore yourself. This can be the chance to take up a hobby you have always wanted to do, take time to learn the language or study something new. On the other hand, perhaps it is time to kick back and really take some time to relax.

MONEY

There is also the issue of money. I went from earning my own salary to my husband being the only income earner when we first relocated, and it took some time to stop feeling like a 1950's housewife. In hindsight I was still working freelance and studying but the change from being financially independent was a hard one at first. For many people, leaving their own careers behind to follow their partner's new job may set them back, and this is something you need to think about before making the move. Is there a way you can continue with your work on a contract or freelance basis in your new home or are there opportunities for you to start to forge your career on new soil? Again in many countries there are spouse care organisations or at least Facebook groups for women (as more often than not it is women in this situation) to help in this adjustment.

Another aspect of money is that you may find that your household income is affected by the move, especially if you go from a two income household to one. It is important in the early stages of negotiating your new salaries and packages that you have an idea about how much your new living expenses will be. I have had a couple of clients through my relocation service who decided not to move to Copenhagen as they couldn't have the lifestyle they enjoyed on the salary and tax regime here. Of course there is more to life than money but it makes a real difference if you are feeling a constant compromise. If you really want to make the move you can find economies but you need to be sure this is worth it.

SHOPPING

It may seem trivial but shopping, especially for groceries, can be one of the biggest adjustments when moving to a new country. If you are moving from Australia, the US or the UK your expectations of shopping will certainly be different to the reality in your new country. Most European cities will not offer the large scale supermarkets where you can buy everything under one roof once a week. Reasons for this will vary. Culturally, in some countries people will prefer to buy their food a few times a week to have the freshest produce. In cities where fewer people drive cars a 'big shop' is not physically possible. Another reason is a practical one as building space is simply not available. Choice is another aspect of shopping to which it can take time to adjust. It can be argued that the volume of products carried in big supermarkets in the UK and US doesn't actually mean more choice. Most people probably buy the same things each week anyway. However, there will be a perception that smaller supermarkets offer less choice; but in time this can become refreshing. Less time on decisions in the supermarket aisle equals more time to enjoy life.

More on shopping in Chapter Sixteen.

PRICES

It is very easy to get caught up in the comparison of prices of things between your home country and your new country, and sometimes finding that the new place falls short by seeming very expensive. Budgeting is important but so is realism. This is what stuff costs so unless you can find an alternative source through friends and family or the Internet, you need to decide if you want something or not and pay the price. The best way to make your money go further is to find the best prices for things in your new city and where to buy them. There is a lot less snobbery about 'discount' or 'budget' supermarkets outside of the UK so always consider these choices if they are available.

It is advice given in Chapter Twelve by many other expats but constant comparison with your old life will always prevent you from fully embracing your new life.

CHAPTER 8

technology and its role in relocation

I moved to Copenhagen when social media was in its infancy. I was on Facebook but it wasn't like it is today. There were no Facebook groups to join, businesses were not on there so you couldn't follow local places for more information. Instagram was just a twinkle in someone's eye. Blogs were also in their infancy. Smartphones were not available so once you left your house you left the Internet behind – no Google Maps to ease you into a new city.

I make it sound like I moved in Medieval times but it was just nine years ago, however over the last five years, technology has made moving to a new city so much easier. I could argue that it might take some of the excitement of discovery away but at the same time it makes cities more accessible and the settling in period a lot easier. In many ways using technology helps significantly with the issue of language barriers.

So how can technology help in your relocation?

BEFORE YOU MOVE
GOOGLE MAPS AND STREET VIEW

Even before you move and you are back in your home country you can 'walk' around possible areas by using Google Street View. Depending on the country you are moving to it does vary how much you can actually see. For example, Germany is very reluctant to have too much detail on Street View, whereas other countries are more relaxed. If you have some possible addresses or areas in mind you can get a good idea of them – is there a lot of graffiti, are there lots of bars, is the street nice and leafy? – the list goes on.

RENTAL PORTALS

Even if you have someone helping you find a home, getting familiar with the rental portals for your new city can really help in finding the right home. You can see the kind of places available for your budget and you can start to adjust expectations you may have or start to get excited about your possibilities.

SOCIAL MEDIA

Start to join some expat Facebook groups but be prepared to take a lot with a very large pinch of salt. You can start to connect with people. You can also look for events taking places in your new city and follow local businesses. It all gives you a solid starting point for when you move. If you are on Instagram check out some of the popular hashtags for your new city and start following some of the popular Instagrammers. I love Instagram, not just because it is so visual, but because it is a very positive platform. Of course Social Media really comes into its own once you are on the ground, but laying foundations before you move is a big help.

TRANSLATOR TOOLS

When faced with websites in a foreign language it is easy to start to feel frustrated, which is why browsers like Google Chrome, which automatically translate websites into your own language, are a massive time saver. Back in the day I carried a small English-Danish dictionary around with me but your phone does this for you now and can even speak the words to you.

ONCE YOU HAVE MOVED
TRAVEL

This is the most obvious one. Most cities offer online travel planners where you can plug in your starting point and your end location and they work it out for you. Couple this with following your route on Google Maps or similar, and it should help you not get lost in a new city.

Mobile tickets are also widely available so you can pay for your travel from your phone and never get caught out with the wrong ticket.

Stuck somewhere on foot and lost again? Google Maps are your friend. It is worth spending some time working on a map of your own, adding places you discover so you can return to them another time. I recall finding an Indian restaurant down a swarm of streets in the oldest part of Copenhagen and spending a good half hour dragging my increasingly hungry husband up and down streets insisting it was 'just around the corner'.

Taxi apps are also well worth looking into if they are available in your new city. Then you don't have to worry about the language barrier if you need to book a taxi.

KEEPING IN TOUCH

Of course, the obvious way that technology really helps in relocation and settling in is the power of things like Skype and FaceTime to keep visually in touch with friends and family. If you get a Skype In number it can often be much cheaper than having a landline put into your new place.

ONLINE SHOPPING

This covers both local and remote shopping.

If you love books then Amazon and similar websites will be the best way to access them in your own language, as it is unlikely that you will find huge selections of books in your new city. You may find that your prefer to buy other items from online shops rather than pay local prices or only having the local selection. This is a good thing to a certain extent, but you need to be wary of delivery costs and possible extra taxes you may need to pay. Also, money spent in the local economy is worth a lot more than just the face value of the goods.

Online grocery shopping and takeaway ordering is increasingly available in the major cities worldwide. Ordering your groceries online can help when you don't speak the language yet and are unsure of what your supermarket offers. You can either use a translator tool or use it as an opportunity to learn some vocabulary as the goods are usually accompanied by a useful picture.

Secondly, home delivery for takeaways. Many cities have takeaway services that cover many different takeaways and restaurants, and food can be ordered from a central website. Just take care in checking the delivery time you have booked. The first time I used the system in Berlin I accidentally ordered my evening sushi to come immediately, just after I had finished my lunch!

MONEY MATTERS

Many banking apps will offer an English version as this is easier to offer than full Internet banking. Also, having a currency converter on your phone will help in the early days when you still need to convert prices so you understand how much money you are spending.

REVIEW WEBSITES

Crowd sourced review websites are an excellent starting point to find the popular places in your city. Yelp is a brilliant one as it features almost every conceivable type of business you may need to use and covers tons of cities.

Trust Pilot, currently available in 24 countries, is a community based review website that allows you to make informed choices about what and where to purchase products.

Of course, these kinds of websites are only as strong as the community that uses them.

MAGAZINES ON TABLETS

If you are a big consumer of magazines you will find they cost an inflated price outside the country of publication, sometime almost three times the amount. If you have an iPad or other tablet you can use apps such as Zinio and Issuu to read your favourite magazines at a much cheaper cost, and at times even for free.

CHAPTER 9

my relocation story – berlin

Relocating can be very exciting and scary and so many other things in-between, but it is very important to take care of yourself, both emotionally and physically, during this time.

I had a great experience when I moved to Copenhagen the first time in 2008, but my experience with the move to Berlin was very different. If you read my blog or know me you will know that I am very positive about life in Copenhagen and for me it is a great place to live, however I know that not everyone's experience is the same.

I wanted to share my personal and painful experience of moving from Copenhagen to Berlin. We were settled in Copenhagen and my son was just 18 months old, life was good and we were making plans for our future when my husband's company dropped a bombshell. They were closing their entire operation in Denmark and everyone would be losing their jobs. He had been with the company for almost 14 years and was valued. They gave him (and us) the Easter weekend to consider taking a position in their Berlin office. I remember walking around Frederiksberg with our son sleeping in the pram talking and talking about what to do. We made a decision that seemed right at the time (and even in hindsight it was still the right one at that time with the information we had available and without a crystal ball), and he took the offer to move. The financial crisis

45

meant that jobs were not so easy to get and with a child and no other income coming in it seemed like a no-brainer. I thought, 'How bad can it be?'

Things started moving quickly as they wanted him to start in September. We started to search online for apartments and we were allocated a relocation consultant on the ground in Berlin. She appeared disorganised from the start and didn't seem to really listen or understand what we needed. We had an idea of the areas we wanted to live in as Berlin is a big city and we didn't want to live too far from my husband's workplace. She gave us no advice on other neighbourhoods, despite the fact that the ones we were looking at were very popular. After a disastrous week-long trip to find a home in August, where she walked us around a number of unsuitable properties in over 30 degree temperatures, we were still no closer to finding a home. Nothing really met with the criteria we had discussed and she didn't acknowledge this. The icing on the cake was when she showed us a dark and gloomy apartment metres away from a suspended busy railway line and declared how much she liked the sound of trains. A silent screaming doesn't even begin to describe my inward reaction.

From about this time I started to lose weight but continued to try and have a positive outlook. With the time of my husband's new start date looming it seemed we had little choice but to arrange temporary housing, have our belongings stored and look for something once we were there. My son and I stayed at my parents' place in France for a week whilst my husband oversaw the packers and moved to the temporary place. The reality hit me one night at my parents' place. My son was asleep and I just sat at the kitchen table with huge tears falling from my eyes. I didn't actually cry or make a noise, I just wept. I felt rootless – we had no home to go to or to go back to.

Once settled in the temporary housing a week later, we realised the relocation consultant had messed up again. We had a choice of several temporary places and she had pushed us towards this one as in her opinion it was best for families. It was located in a former Stasi office block, and whilst the little apartment was functional, it was soulless. It was also impractical for us. The wifi was hopeless (our lifeline for finding an apartment as our relocation consultant seemed to be half-hearted in her service to us), and it was located in a less than nice part of town, as was illustrated by the drug addicts hanging around outside the local supermarket and shooting up in the lift at the U Bahn station. We needed tokens for the washing machines and the office was open for a tiny window of time every week to buy them, and despite the building being full of non-Germans, the woman in the office refused to even attempt to meet me halfway with any English.

My weight continue to plummet and I started to have issues with tinnitus (which I now know was brought on by stress). I would sit in the evening after an exhausting day of fruitless apartment searches and trying to keep some level of normalcy for my son and just weep. I wanted to go home but as my husband kindly said, this is home now, we can't go back.

I realised that when I had thought, 'How bad can it be?', I had no idea. We continued to look for apartments, many found by us and some by the relocation consultant. We started to learn that you couldn't get excited or attached to them as at every turn we were losing out to others. We had no idea why and how to make us more appealing as tenants (I feel become less British may have helped). We later realised that we could have afforded a lot more on rent but the person who should have advised us on this didn't.

We were looking at still being in the temporary housing after Christmas and the thought was devastating. We had offers of many places to go for Christmas but the thought of returning to the Stasi block in the harshest part of the year sent me even further down. I had spoken to a number of other wives in the building and they all told the same story of impossible apartment searches, and most were many months further down the line. They told me to do as they had done and get anti-depressants from the doctor located in the block. I think I was probably the only expat wife there I spoke to who wasn't on 'happy' pills.

We found an apartment online way out in former East Berlin in Pankow, which at that time was not fashionable. It was huge, within our price range and still available. I went and checked out the area and my gut was screaming, No!'. At that time it was a sad and slightly rundown part of town and still very 'East', but I was tired and depressed and we needed somewhere to call home. The apartment was lovely but in time I learnt that you can make an average place home, but without the right area and local amenities you will struggle.

We put an application in for the place and we heard by the end of the day that we were successful. Obviously, Pankow wasn't on many people's list of number one places to live and the fact the apartment was under a busy flight path probably had something to do with it.

We arranged for our stuff to come from Denmark and over a week I spent every evening until late unpacking the place so we could move in by December. I was weighing in at 8st by then, my ears were constantly ringing, I was often too tired to keep awake during the day, despite sleeping at night. We left the temporary housing and moved in to our new place. The first evening there I went out to find the local supermarket which, despite looking on the map, I simply couldn't find. I walked around the dark streets becoming increasingly hysterical. I remembered the little shopping mall nearby and went there to look for groceries. I walked into this excessively bright mall just as a dreadful talent show was going on and had the first of many panic attacks. I called my husband and finally made my way home with nothing to eat. I think this is when I hit rock bottom.

My husband's work sent him to China for a few weeks and my mum came to stay. She was horrified by the state I was in. I had tried to conceal from family and friends just how tough these months had been. After giving me a lot of love that week and helping with the settling in, I felt stronger. I made an appointment with my new GP to talk about my ear problem and she immediately recognised that I was suffering from some kind of physical and emotional breakdown. She didn't reach for her prescription pad, but talked to me. She made me come and see her every week to talk and have a check-up. The kindness she showed me was the first time I felt anyone in Berlin was trying to help.

As we entered a new year things started to improve, but I knew this was never a place for us. I made the best of it, we joined music classes for my son, we explored, I made friends, I started a blog and kept busy. I still struggled with the lack of patience of Berliners when I tried to speak German, yet they wouldn't or couldn't speak English to me; the level of rudeness around me; the dirtiness of the city, the theft of things from my buggy, the extremes of weather (minus 15 degrees C in the winter and 35 degrees C in the summer). When, just a year from his first redundancy, my husband lost his job again we made the easy decision to take the money and run as fast as we could back to Copenhagen.

I can blame a lot of people for the situation we were in and I wish, in hindsight, I had felt more equipped to take more control over it. But there were many practical things I learned, and I also found out what was important to us as a family and a couple. I unjustly blamed my husband for the situation at my darkest moments, yet he still stuck with it and supported me, even though I am sure he felt some of the same emotions and also didn't know what to do to change things or how to help me.

Gradually, things got better. I am not sure what changed but something did, and I learnt a lot about what was important to me and to us as a family over that time. There are many legacies from that time that we are still dealing with, but as time passes so does the negative baggage I gathered during those eighteen months. I also gained strength from the experience and once the bitterness receded, I can see a pattern of how I let things get so bad and how to fight this if it ever happens again. In the next chapter I share the lessons I learnt and how they can help others in a similar situation.

CHAPTER 10

lessons in being kind to yourself

From my tough experience in Berlin I can understand how much isolation and the lack of having a concrete place to call home can really bash you down. It is important to see that a relocation isn't always a bed of roses, and that some very simple things can help. Being kind to yourself is the most important thing. There will be people who find the move to a new place simple, but even if you do there are some days when things are anything but easy. The feeling of isolation is one that expats regularly suffer from, and it is easy to get into a spiral of isolation and loneliness. There are ways you can take control and fight this.

GET OUT OF THE HOUSE EVERY DAY

I forced myself to go out somewhere every day with my son – whether it was a walk in the park, a wander around the local market, to a child-friendly cafe or to run an errand. In hindsight, when we were living in temporary housing in Berlin, I pushed myself too much and this led to some of the exhaustion I suffered, but I still believe that getting out of the house is essential and once you are in a permanent location helps you find your feet in your new area. It is essential for your health and sanity as it serves as a distraction from everything that can be overwhelming you, and gives you an immediate focus.

JOIN GROUPS

Especially if you are a parent at home with a child, joining groups gives you a purpose and the chance to meet other people. We joined groups and went to music classes, and even though I wasn't my normal self I made efforts to make friends or at least speak to people.

You may not make bosom buddies but you will get to speak to others. There are loads of

Meetup groups in every city, covering a multitude of interests. Picking a couple to join gives you the chance to do something you like and also the chance to talk to like-minded people, at least for a few hours.

ASK FOR HELP

I am terrible at this but the Berlin experience made me realise I need to be better at it. It is amazing how many people are happy and willing to help you if you ask. You may find some people will be less willing to help, but most will.

Sharing worries and problems really does make them easier to deal with – I know it's a cliché, but it is true. Speak to your doctor if you are feeling down and talk to your loved ones; they will want to help you even if they too are struggling with your move. I made the choice to hide how hard I found our move to Berlin from loved ones far away, but I should have been more open and got more support. Don't box yourself in with your fears and worries. Let your partner in on how you are feeling. They will probably be feeling some, if not all, of the same emotions and you can support each other.

Join online groups for other expats or parents in your new city. Talk to baristas in your local coffee house – sounds weird but these guys are usually friendly and have their finger on the pulse of your neighbourhood, and will always have a smile for you. No matter how tough it seems, you need to get out there even if it is only in a virtual way at first.

TAKE ONE STEP AT A TIME BUT STAY FOCUSED

You won't be able to do everything at once, especially if you are struggling emotionally.

Each day or week make a list of the top few things you need to do, things that must be done even if they seem really trivial, like walk to the local supermarket and see what they sell. Get hold of something you need to make daily life easier, for example, go online and download public transport maps. Locate all the amenities you need in your local area and then spread out this research further afield. Think: local hospital accident and emergency department, local taxi firms, supermarkets that open longer hours, pharmacies, hairdressers that speak your language, florists for brightening up your space, DIY stores, local playgrounds, parks, coffee shops. This research also helps get you out of the house but equally can be done online. It also means you if you need this information quickly you are not rushing to find it.

DO FUN STUFF

Sometimes, when the going gets tough, the fun things fall by the wayside. Enjoyable activities enrich your life, and although these things may not seem as essential as finding a permanent home or unpacking boxes they will make you more comfortable in the long run. Find a local museum to visit for a few hours (with kids or alone), go to a local coffee shop and order a big slice of cake and people-watch. Buy some magazines that interest you. You may not be able to read much if you can't speak the language, but the pictures are fun to look at and you get an idea of the new culture you live in, especially when it comes to fashion.

DON'T GIVE UP!

There is a cliché, 'This too shall pass', and whilst at the time it feels like a prison sentence if you are struggling with a relocation, I promise you it gets better, it really does. After a time things seem easier, more familiar and less daunting – you may still not like where you live but maybe you will hate it a little less all the time. For some this takes a few months, for others a few years, and it is gradual. All of a sudden you will be looking back on the tough times as a distant memory, and you won't even see when the turning point was but it will come, I promise.

CHAPTER 11

making friends and fighting isolation

One of the biggest fears that people, especially women, have when relocating to a new country is how they will find and make friends. I would argue that the situation could be similar if you moved to a new city in your own country, as people there will already have existing friendships and groups that can often be difficult to penetrate.

One of the benefits of being an expat is that you are likely to be, at least at the beginning, moving in the same circles as other expats and this can help in making friends.

IMPORTANCE OF CONNECTION

It may seem obvious but unless you are putting yourself in places where you will meet people and being outgoing and friendly to people you do meet, you won't find making friends easy. People won't be seeking you out so you need to put in the legwork initially. Language school is one of the best places to meet new people if you are not working in an office environment. Secondly, look at your hobbies and interests and join groups, either virtual or real, that are about these.

Even before you move you can start to make connections with people by joining Facebook groups based in your new area, and making an effort to engage with people in these groups. Start threads and conversations and join in with ones already going on. It will make establishing a connection with people in real life much easier.

EXPAT VS LOCAL FRIENDS

There is a big difference between the types of friendships you will forge with expats and those with locals.

Let's start with expats. In the main, many expats you meet will be living in the country for a shorter and specific period of time. If they are seasoned expats they will be used to making friends quickly with others as time is of the essence. You may find that your new expat friends will share personal details about their lives much quicker than you are used to, and you may become fast friends. It is important to remember that this group of friends will be very transitional and situational, and you will get used to saying goodbye a lot. Depending on how long you plan to stay in the country, the ways this kind of friendship affects you can vary as you may be the one to be leaving after a few years.

Then there are seasoned expats, those who are not actually expats in the traditional sense but people who have left their own country to settle on a permanent or long term basis. These people will often already have strong groups of friends, but will be open to newcomers as they recall what it was like for them. They will take things a little slower but are great people to add to your circle as they will have longer term knowledge to share, and are less likely to be heading off to a new place any time soon.

Finally, locals. This is the hardest nut to crack but one that is very worthwhile. In some places, Copenhagen being a prime example, many people will still be living close to old friends and family. They will already have a very strong network and groups of friends, and in fairness why should they go out of their way to make you their new friend? You are most likely to meet local people in your apartment building or street. By putting in the time to introduce yourself, say hello, chat, help out (if applicable), say yes to invitations, extend invitations (but expect them to be politely refused) and be generally friendly, you will gradually make a few but very reliable friends. It takes time, and you will usually find that these people won't be your best buddies, but they will be fun and will help you out.

It is good to have a combination of all of the above types of people in your circle.

SAME NATIONALITY DOESN'T MEAN FRIENDS

One thing I have noticed, and particularly in French retired expat circles, is that you will often see people together who would never have been friends in their home countries. There could be a positive reason for this: when you move somewhere new you lose some of your previous reservations and judgements about others, and take them more at face value and common interests.

But I think in some cases people gravitate to others from their own country almost as a life raft. They speak your language and they understand your cultural references, but it is important to take care with making friends with anyone just to have friends. Simply being friends with other Brits (or whatever your nationality) can stop you from expanding your experiences in a new country. After all, if you wanted to be friends with folk from only your own country, wouldn't you just stay there?

Choose friends that share your interests and ideals for longer lasting bonds.

BEING HONEST ABOUT FRIENDSHIP

This follows on from my point above. You need to think to yourself about what kinds of friends you want to make. There can often be different levels of friends (almost like a pyramid) and it is important to manage your expectations of each level.

Firstly, at the bottom of the pyramid is basically anyone you have met more than a couple of times and with whom your paths cross a lot. These would be people from your language school, workplace, school or daycare (if you are parent). There will be many of them, and you will most probably have a chat when you see them and be starting to get to know them on a superficial basis. It is a bit like starting university, when you make friends with everyone and find yourself asking and replying to the same questions over and over. This stage is important to find who are your 'tribe'.

Next up will be people from the first level who you have more in common with. Perhaps you begin to socialise with them beyond the initial meeting place. These are the people who will start to be your proper friends or your 'tribe'. Some of these will make it up to the next level and be the people you share more about your life, joys, worries and things you need help with.

Finally, at the apex will be the few good friends you have made, that you know you can call on for help at any time, who will be fun to go out with in a relaxed manner and just have a good time.

The speed at which people get to the apex depends on a lot of things. You may find that you spend the first few months in your new home with just a ton of people on the first level, but that is OK. Lasting friendships take time and good friendships are not made overnight.

A TWO-WAY STREET

I often hear new expats moan that local people aren't friendly and are not interested in making friends with them, but friendship is a two-way street. There needs to be a strong element of reciprocity in friendship, and even more so when you are the newcomer. Make sure you are not always taking and asking for favours with nothing in return.

The second Christmas we lived in Copenhagen, we invited everyone in our building to our apartment one afternoon for mulled wine and mince pies. It was a great way to break the ice and also to show our welcoming side. We made sure we always pitched in on the apartment building clear up days and after the serious citywide floods of 2011. We also made sure we got involved in building activities such as the lighting of the communal Christmas tree.

HAVING KIDS HELPS

Having children is a massive help in connecting with and making friends. You can take your child to a music group and meet people, you can strike up conversations with interesting looking fellow mums using the children as a starting point. There are tons more places geared up to getting children together than adults and you can cash in on this. And if the worst comes to the worst at least your child will speak to you if no one else does!

BE GENUINE

It is very easy to find yourself falling into a mould to try and fit in with a new circle of friends, but stay true to yourself and be genuine. This will help you make more real and true friends. I am generally quite outgoing and friendly but I do have a quiet side, which I don't hide. It is important that people have the chance to meet the real you.

Of course, moving to a new country does give you the chance to perhaps reinvent yourself a little. We can also find ourselves outwardly becoming a certain way or showing a certain personality to others, when our true personality gets hidden within. Perhaps you have always been creative and this has been stifled a little – now is the time to let that side out and give it a chance to flourish.

CHAPTER 12

advice from other expats

In this chapter I share advice from other expats from around the world (although many are living in Copenhagen). I asked them to give me the one piece of advice they would have found the most valuable when they first relocated.

SHARON RELOCATED TO DENMARK FROM THE UK IN 2013

"Start language classes to build a network."

When I relocated to Denmark from England with my Danish husband and our daughter I quickly realised I would have to adapt to many new things. But most importantly for me, it was enrolling in language classes that really helped me to adapt and feel part of society here. Language school is also a great place to meet new people and start to develop a network, which is so important in Denmark. Most importantly, be patient and keep a positive attitude.

CAROLYN RELOCATED TO DENMARK FROM AUSTRALIA IN 2014

"Join groups and get connected and social."

I didn't expect to make such good friendships whilst here. You always believe that you'll just move for a few years and then move home with no real connections with people, but that's not the case. My piece of advice is to join groups with people that share the same hobbies as you, or play-groups if you have children. They keep you connected and social in your new location.

POLLY RELOCATED TO DENMARK FROM THE UK IN 2014

"Use your head not your heart when finding a home."

When house hunting, make sure that you remember to envisage your own life when you're looking around properties, rather than being seduced by the lifestyle of the occupant. When we moved to Denmark, we looked around an apartment that was beautifully decorated and selling the Danish idyll. The stunning furniture, fairy lights and candles totally blinded us to impracticalities of the apartment. We've made a success out of our apartment regardless, but both feel that we might have found life easier if we'd picked a place to live using our heads rather than our hearts.

STUART RELOCATED TO DENMARK FROM AUSTRALIA IN 2014

"Be flexible and don't try and recreate your home country."

Don't try and recreate your home country in your new place of residence. Don't try to achieve the house and the food you have at home because it stops you from being flexible with what's available to you. Pay attention to the way things are done in the environment around you because they usually have evolved over a long period of time for a reason, for example 'hygge' – how to survive cold dark winters with comfort.

PETER MOVED TO FRANCE FROM ENGLAND IN 2005

*"Don't ask if someone speaks your language
but say you can't speak theirs."*

Mirror the culture around you and ask for help in a way that is acceptable in your new country – in some places you can be blunter than others and in some you need to be more humble. For example, don't ask if someone speaks your language but say you can't speak theirs. Try and use what you can in their language and they are more likely to meet you half way. This is especially important in countries like France and Germany. And remember it's not necessarily easy for them to speak your language to you.

SARITA MOVED TO COPENHAGEN FROM INDIA IN 2012

*"Enjoy the journey of discovering a new country,
its people, its customs and culture."*

Saunter, don't rush into a relationship with your host country. Give both yourself and the people around you the time to understand each other. Don't be in a hurry to set expectations or make judgements. Enjoy the journey of discovering a new country, its people, its customs and culture.

KATIE RELOCATED FROM ENGLAND TO COPENHAGEN IN SUMMER 2015

*"When everything is overwhelming, foreign and confusing, it can
make a world of difference to slip into your own sheets
at the end of the day."*

It can be worth taking on a short term rental before committing to something more long term, but make sure you take a few small boxes of things that make you feel like this new home is your home. Not just the clothes and the essentials, but a couple of items which connect your present to your past, and make you feel like you're not standing still in somebody else's house. My husband and I packed our adored bed linen, a few choice books, and the hearty casserole dish we use every Sunday, which was a wedding present. When everything is overwhelming, foreign and confusing, it can make a world of difference to slip into your own sheets at the end of the day.

ANNE MOVED TO COPENHAGEN FROM IRELAND IN 2012 AND RETURNED TO DUBLIN IN 2016.

"Embrace the opportunity you have been given."

My advice is probably more relevant to those who leave work to follow a partner overseas, as this has been my experience. It can be very daunting to lose your 'work self' and the sense of identity that this has given you. But there is great freedom in reconnecting with who you are outside of your work identity. Embrace the opportunity you have been given. Think of all the things you would like to be doing if you weren't working full time. Now is the time to do them.

POLINA MOVED TO DENMARK 12 YEARS AGO FROM RUSSIA

"An ongoing, proactive communication is the first key to a pleasant time in a new country."

I would highly recommend seeking out a local community of expatriates from your home country. Most importantly, there will be a long term expatriate in nearly every group. That person can provide a short introduction to practicalities, cultural difference, traditions and so on. When I first moved here I found a Russian community and can admit that this has helped me to avoid depression related to relocation. I would say that an ongoing proactive communication is the first key to a pleasant time in a new country.

KATE, FROM THE US LIVING IN GERMANY SINCE 2009

"It's amazing how friendly and helpful strangers can be, especially if they are expats too."

Connect on social media! I don't know what expats did before the Internet. Social media, blogs and the rest of it, are invaluable ways to meet and learn from others when you are half a world away from the life and people you know. It is through social media that I've really connected with the people who have become an incredible support system in my adopted home country, and all over the world. Seek out people who are similar to you and see what they like, where they go and even solicit advice. It's amazing how friendly and helpful strangers can be, especially if they are expats too.

NATASHA MOVED FROM THE UK TO KUALA LUMPUR IN 2014

"Stop comparing! It'll only be through accepting differences and being open to change that you'll ever be able to fully settle and call where you have migrated to home."

I, and the majority of expats I've met, have been guilty of the phrase, 'I love it here, but…' after which we make some comparison to life back home. Of course, this is normal and, most of the time, it's trivial but it can be a slippery slope and, left unchecked, comparisons can become criticism. Once critical of the place you've come to, it's difficult to see anything in a positive light and it's easy to stop making the effort.

Remember, you're living in a new country – of course things are going to be different. It'll only be through accepting these differences and being open to change that you'll ever be able to fully settle and call where you have migrated to home.

ALEXANDRA "COOKIE" MOVED TO COPENHAGEN IN 2015 AND IS FROM THE USA

"I would tell someone who is new to a country to enjoy each day as it comes – especially in terms of the weather."

There is a Danish saying, "There is no such thing as bad weather, only bad clothing!" I would go so far as to add a bad attitude to that combination as well. Keeping that in mind, if you are dressed for the elements and have a positive outlook and happy attitude, you will never have a bad day, So when it is sunny make sure to go outside, soak it up and when it is cold and rainy dress accordingly. Most of all, enjoy yourself in your new environs.

PAOLA MOVED TO COPENHAGEN FROM ITALY IN 2012

*"Volunteering and learning the language were two
other important steps to build networks."*

I came to Copenhagen following my husband's new job. I soon learnt that networking is the key. Danes are tribal and knowing somebody in the right place is the best way in. Volunteering and learning the language were two other important steps to build networks. I have learnt so much, and got to know the country I'm living in and great people that in time have become good friends.

MALIHA, ORIGINALLY FROM PAKISTAN, HAS RELOCATED TWICE, TO LONDON AND COPENHAGEN.

*"The inability to land a satisfying job is not always your fault so
you need to be kinder to yourself during the job search
and have an open mind."*

Very few relocation resources talk how to deal with the disappointment of leaving a good job behind when following a spouse's career and not finding something suitable in the new country. My advice would be to prepare yourself mentally that the ideal job may be hard to come by. And also be prepared to accept something totally different or move several steps behind professionally. Understand that countries are very different and so are the job markets. And most of all, the inability to land a satisfying job is not always your fault so you need to be kinder to yourself during the job search and have an open mind.

CHAPTER 13

learning the language

Many expats choose not to learn the language of the country they are living in and there are a multitude of reasons why this decision is made, but I really believe that learning at least some language of your new country helps you feel happier and more settled.

BENEFITS OF SMALL TALK AND WORDS FOR FOOD

It makes life much more pleasant if you know enough of the local language to make small talk with people, read adverts and understand the basics of what you see and hear around you. I understand for many people who are only relocating for a short period of time the commitment of formal lessons doesn't seem to be a good use of your time but there are a number of free or inexpensive resources available for many languages to give you a quick taster.

One of the most important things you need to understand is food words. A wander around the supermarket can really help out with this and getting a decent translator tool on your smart phone helps too.

FIGHTING ISOLATION

We may think that English is very widely spoken in the world but you will often find this is not always the case. If every day you are finding simply the basics of daily life are a struggle due to a language barrier, this is even more reason to learn a little.

One of the reasons I felt unsettled in Berlin was the fact that my German was very basic and people in my neighbourhood were unable, or perhaps unwilling, to help me out by trying to speak English or understand my pronunciation. I became scared to even try to speak my basic German due to the reaction I got, and this became counterproductive and did nothing to help me feel less isolated. I stuck with it though and by the time I left Germany I knew a lot of vocabulary (not all that useful) and was able to structure basic sentences.

EASY WAYS TO PICK UP VOCAB

Children's books, especially stories you may be familiar with, or very simple stories are a great place to start. Don't be embarrassed about what you are reading. I recall reading the most boring books when I was first learning Danish and they all seemed so tough to read, so I went to the library and got a Famous Five book in Danish. I was immediately transported back to Kirin Island and forgot I was actually learning.

Another a great way to start reading a language is choosing magazines about something that interests you. The best advice I can give you is to find subjects that you enjoy and seek out materials to read or listen to around these things – whether it is fashion, sport or technology.

ONLINE COURSES

If you have time before you move, online courses are the way to go. I have tried out a few online courses that seem fun and easy to pick up a few basics. I can also recommend Rosetta Stone – although the financial commitment is high, it does yield results and is fun and interactive at the same time. Duolingo is my current favourite for online language learning and it is fun, free and you learn quickly.

CLASSROOM BASED LEARNING

There is no substitute for classroom based learning, either in a class or with an individual tutor. I had a great experience when I first moved to Copenhagen as the government provide free lessons for holders of CPR numbers (you pay a basic fee for books and examinations, and you get more than your money's worth). The structure of the course that I took was great. The first module is all about speaking and getting a feel for what seems at first to be a very complex language. It gives students confidence and helps you stick around for the harder modules.

Most language schools in major cities will offer a variety of taught courses to fit around different kinds of students, whether it is a fast intensive course, longer but still relatively intensive, blended online and class based classes or evening classes that fit around your life. Your life and expectations will have a bearing on how you approach your learning.

GREAT FOR NETWORKING

There are more benefits than just learning a new language. Language school is also a great way to make new friends who are all in a similar situation to you and come from a diverse geographical background. They are all keen to learn the language and also about the new culture. I met almost all of my good friends here in the first few months at language school and built a network of people from this.

ASK FOR LESSONS AS PART OF YOUR EMPLOYMENT PACKAGE

If you are moving as an accompanying spouse or you have a job with a big company yourself, try and get language lessons included in your new employment package for either you and/or your partner, especially if you are moving to a country that does not offer government subsidised classes. We have been lucky enough to have been offered these when moving both to Denmark and Germany.

melanie haynes

BE FEARLESS AND GIVE IT A GO

My advice is, that if you can spare a few months of mornings or evenings, take the opportunity to have some language lessons either in a classroom setting or online. No matter how painful it feels, use what you learn out there with real people as it is the only way you will get the pronunciation right and gain confidence in learning the language. I almost stalked my neighbours to try out my new skills, which must have been very tedious when my conversations were at the level of a six year old. It can take an element of bravery to put yourself out there so publicly, but in most instances local people will welcome your attempts to speak their language and hopefully reciprocate in English if you start to struggle.

CHAPTER 14

times of the year

I t is easy to assume that our experiences of the ebb and flow of the year are universal, but whilst it might seem that moving from one Western country to another should be seamless, the reality is far from it.

PUBLIC HOLIDAYS AND SCHOOL BREAKS

Have you ever been on holiday out of season thinking you will avoid school children, and then spend your relaxing break surrounded by German school kids? European school holidays rarely match up with UK or US ones. For example, the French finish for the summer at the start of July and go back at the beginning of September, Danes finish at the end of June and are back by the second week of August, but in the UK summer holidays start at the end of July and continue until the beginning of September. It's important to get these dates in your calendar at the start of the year if you are planning to visit friends and family, or indeed have them visit you over the school holidays.

Public holidays are also going to be different in your new country. Depending on the dominant religion of the country and other traditional celebrations there will be a completely different calendar of free days than you may be used to. It is also worth noting that if a public holiday falls on a Thursday as they often do in mainland Europe some schools and daycare places will also shut on the Friday. There are tons of resources on this online so a quick search on the internet for your new country's public holidays is helpful.

You may also find in Northern Europe that many celebrations are held on the eve of the actual day so, for example, Christmas is celebrated on the 24th in Scandinavian countries and Germany (amongst others). Check shop opening times for forthcoming public holidays so you don't get caught out as in many countries there is less of an 'open all hours' lifestyle.

WEATHER AND THE ENVIRONMENT

Most Europeans enjoy talking about the weather, and is there any wonder when it has such a massive impact on our everyday lives? Since living in Northern Europe I am the proud possessor of a number of items I would either have turned my nose up at when I was living in the UK, or wouldn't even have known of their existence.

CLOTHING

If you are moving to Southern Europe this will be irrelevant, but anyone living any further north than the top of Italy will need to think about clothes for all weathers, especially if you are living a car-free lifestyle. As they say here, 'There is no such thing as bad weather, just bad clothing.'

KEEPING DRY

The main things you will need to combat the rain (and which I now wear regularly around town) are waterproof trousers, wellies (the selection in Denmark is uber stylish) or waterproof boots and a long waterproof coat that goes over your waterproof trousers.

Finally, and most shameful, is a waterproof poncho which make me look like a cross between a bag of rubbish and a huge bat. Again, if you want to spend money on this item of clothing you can look slightly (but not much) more stylish. But I am dry, warm and my hair still looks reasonable after the school run on my cargo bike. On the subject of hair, a selection of beanies or woolly hats of varying weights depending in the season (excluding the summer, I hope) are worth having.

KEEPING WARM

Winters in Northern Europe vary from being magical to brutal with snow and icy winds, so a proper warm coat, and not a fashion coat, is a necessity for the winter. Once the mercury falls it seems as if Copenhagen is sponsored by The North Face and Berlin by Jack Wolfskin but there is a reason, and that is these are the companies that know their stuff. I favour a good quality coat, with a hood, that covers my thighs – style and warmth at once.

Boots are something else to consider. I bought a pair of Sorrel boots, fur-lined with a rubber sole and amazing grip that comes up over the sides of the boot to keep it dry in the snow. I bought these boots eight years ago, have worn them every day for at least four months of each of those years and they still look almost new. They were expensive but worth it.

As I mention above, you will need a hat for the winter as well as a few pairs of gloves. You will lose one at some point, and it is advisable to have a wide selection of these in varying weights. For the spring/autumn get some hand warmers with fingers out made from lightweight wool. Then there are proper basic, fashion woolly gloves for a tiny window of time before you need to move into warmer options, such as Icelandic wool mittens. These are amazing and are semi-waterproof thanks to the natural lanolin in the wool. You shouldn't wash these, and I can vouch for their moisture repelling nature after dropping them in a muddy puddle on a farm to find them dry and clean in less than an hour. Finally, some thick windproof and waterproof gloves or mittens for the depths of winter. These can be picked up in the outdoor sections of most sports shops.

CHILDREN'S CLOTHING

This is a whole other ball game and an expensive one as children have a nasty habit of growing out of stuff by the next season. Checking out decent second hand stores, flea markets and online sales sites can help reduce the cost, as can looking in the clothing sections of supermarkets. My advice from life in Denmark, Germany and France is to buy early or risk not having much or any choice later on.

This is the basic winter clothes list you need for living in Northern Europe. If it's your first winter here with children here is a quick checklist of things you need to get:

- Winter jacket
- Snowsuit or above jacket combined with padded trousers
- Winter boots (waterproof, warm and high up the ankles – wellies are not going to cut it)
- Padded gloves or mittens (and clips to attach them to coats)
- Wool gloves
- Vests and leggings (in case it gets properly cold)
- A balaclava style hat. (Many preschools and schools will ask that you don't use scarves for safety but these kind of balaclava hats that come down well below the neck for extra warmth. In my opinion they are very warm and more practical than a hat and scarf combo anyway.)
- Thick warm socks for all and tights for girls

WINTER HEALTH
SKIN AND HAIR CARE

I find that I need to think a lot more about my skincare since living in a cold climate and also spending so much time outside. The change in water in your new country can also have an impact on both skin and hair – I found the water in Berlin very drying, and when I first moved to Copenhagen my skin took a while to adjust to the high levels of calcium in the water.

A decent, rich face cream and lip balm will help stop your skin from drying out in the winter. You will probably find you need to use something much heavier than you would do in the UK or further south. Pharmacies and health food shops often have an excellent selection of winter creams and the staff are very knowledgable. For young children and babies a lanolin based cream which gives their cheeks protection from the wind and cold is an excellent investment. I think the Weleda Weather Protection cream with lanolin is perfect.

VITAMINS

Living in Northern Europe you will find your vitamin D reserves can take a bashing due to the shorter winter days. I always take a general vitamin supplement to boost my immune system from about September to March, and I make sure it has 100% of my daily vitamin D in it. It is easy to find just vitamin D supplements if you don't want to take other vitamins. Lack of vitamin D can have a huge impact both on your health and your energy levels so it is well worth considering, even if you are not normally a vitamin taker.

DAYLIGHT LAMP

You may well have never heard of such things (I certainly hadn't) but a daylight or Seasonal Affective Disorder (SAD) lamp is a lifesaver if you are living somewhere with short days of light in the winter. It replicates natural sunlight and, depending what kind of model you buy, you can set it to wake you up with a gentle sunrise so your body isn't sent into shock when your alarm goes off at what seems to be the middle of the night. You can also have them on during the day and sit by the light for an hour or so to fool your body into thinking it is experiencing real daylight. It really helps people from getting SAD.

CHAPTER 15

using public transport

U sing public transport in a new city, let alone in a new country, can be one of the most daunting things you have to do when you are new to the place, but it is one of the most important to master, quickly. I recall on our proper first morning in Copenhagen, my husband called me to say not to worry about travelling on the bus as they announce the stops. Great for him, but my bus didn't do that and I ended up bouncing up and down for about three stops before I reached mine. Things have moved on in the eight years since then and, with a number of travel apps and transport websites available for smart phones in many major cities, it is much easier to follow your route whilst travelling on buses. It is hard at first but well worth persevering as in many busy cities cars are more trouble than they are worth, and public transport is your friend.

MAPS

The first step is to get hold of a public transport guide for your city – a paper one if possible. This is essential; it will give you a good idea of where things are located and how to get to them before you set off. Maps on smart phones are very useful but it is hard to get a wider overview of your location, which is essential when you are new to a city.

The free city guides here in Copenhagen have all bus routes marked on the maps, but that is the joy of living in a small city. Most tourist information offices in cities will have a city map available, although it may not always be free. But for the price of a few euros you have the city in your hands.

START SMALL

Finding out the main ways to get from your home to work, your children's school and into the city centre are the first things to discover. Take a few journeys when you are not in a rush to get there but at the relevant time of the day. See how long the journey actually takes and also look at the places you pass through, as no doubt there will be somewhere you want to return to another day. Follow on a paper map or on your smart phone map to get your bearings of the area.

ONLINE TRAVEL SITES

Many cities have integrated public transport systems where your tickets cover you for all buses, trains, trams etc., and they will also have a travel website where you can search routes and tickets across all public transport systems. These are very useful up to a point as they lack the human touch and will sometimes offer you a more difficult, albeit quick, route which may involve more changes than someone new to a city needs. My advice is to use these sites in combination with other resources and your own common sense.

TRAVEL TICKETS AND PASSES

Most cities will have some form of season tickets (monthly or annually) or electronic ticket (e.g., Oyster card) to make travelling on public transport cheaper, rather than paying per ride. Pop into your local ticket office at a main station to find out about this and what it covers. You can, of course, search online for it but in the office they can give you a lot more information about what is right for you in the early stages of living in a city. I always believe that real personal contact helps in settling in to a city, and a person can give you more information than a web search.

Never stand at a ticket machine trying to work it out without any research first (been there, done that!). The enormous pressure of working out a new system with a queue of impatient people behind you, even if someone is kind enough to help, is overwhelming and you may end up simply blindly buying something wrong.

DON'T GET FINED!

A great piece of advice I read recently was 'Always pay what you should' when you move to a new country, and transport is the one you really don't want to dodge paying. Saying you are a foreigner or new to a city will not necessarily garner any favour with ticket inspectors.

So you need to find out how things work exactly in your new city. Things may seem the same as you are used to, but a tiny error can result in an expensive fine. For example, in Copenhagen you just buy your ticket and get on with your journey, but in Berlin you need to validate the ticket before you begin to travel, holding the dated ticket is not enough. Travel zones are also important to understand as you can easily drop into a new zone without realising it on unfamiliar routes, and this could result in a fine if you are stopped.

PUBLIC TRANSPORT IS NOT ALWAYS THE BEST OPTION

Walking is often very underrated in cities, especially when you are new and have no idea how far places really are. I remember for years using the Tube in London thinking it was the best way to travel until there were no services one day and I had to walk. I then realised actually how walkable places were and how close together. Sometimes it is better to walk for twenty minutes than cram onto a busy train or bus, plus you get fresh air, exercise and maybe save a bit of money.

TRAVELLING WITH CHILDREN, ANIMALS AND BIKES

In many cities children travel free with an adult so if you are regularly travelling with children find this out early on. Likewise, find out the situation with prams and buggies if you use these. If the transport system in your new city is fairly modern you will find it more user-friendly for prams and buggies. Look out for dedicated carriages on trains and metros, rules on how many prams can go on a bus (two in Copenhagen but more in Berlin), and find out which train and metro stations have lifts. When my son was in a buggy I often had to go one stop further on a journey in Berlin to get to a station with a lift and then walk back.

If you are using public transport with a dog you also need to find out the local rules. Just as an example, in Copenhagen a dog travels free if it can be carried in a dog friendly bag, but has to have a ticket if it walks on. It is not recommended to try and cram your Alsatian dog into a holdall to save money! Likewise, in Germany dogs must be muzzled on public transport no matter how friendly and docile they are.

Bikes can often be taken on trains and metros in cities, but there may be rules about whether you need a bike ticket, and there may also be busy times when bikes are not permitted. Be warned that even if your city has an integrated transport system there still may be different rules for bikes on different sections of the transport network.

CHAPTER 16

shopping

I touched a little on shopping in Chapter Seven but I think it really deserves a chapter of its own as it is the area that is most challenging when relocating, and also the one that needs to be dealt with so that everyday life can continue.

WHERE TO FIND THINGS?

The first piece of advice I would give may seem very obvious but I see time and time again from questions asked in expat forums that it is not. If you are looking to purchase something or find a service (i.e. passport photos) the best piece of advice I can give you is go to the place where you would buy this in your home country. This doesn't always work but eight times out of ten it does. Also, go to the place with the largest selection of shops and you will probably find what you need. Just simply going to shops when you are not looking for a particular thing and browsing can help.

Secondly, ask. And not just on virtual forums but that can help. If you are in a supermarket and can't find something in particular, ask an assistant, that's their job. Even if you can't speak the language well, they may speak English or you can use your translator tool on your phone.

If all else fails there is always mime! I am pretty shameless and when I want some kind of food I will do all I can to get it. On the run up to our first proper Christmas in Berlin I had seen that in the food hall of the big department store on Alexander Platz they were selling whole ducks for roasting. I had a basic grasp of German by then and I had looked up the word for duck. So there I am saying, 'Ich möchte eine Ente' to the grim looking woman on the butcher's counter. Blank look. I repeated it in the time honoured way of raising my voice because, of course, understanding is helped by volume. Still a blank look, and she went to turn away. I am not ashamed to say, as it proved successful, that I then said 'Ente' (duck) again whist making wing-flapping motions with my arms and quacking. I got my duck and she never even raised a smile at my crazy antics. I am not suggesting that you go to these lengths, but a little moderate mime can help.

FOOD SHOPPING

Food shopping can be a challenge when you move to a new country. Of course, we all miss food from home, and whilst there is usually an alternative to be found it is often hard to know where to find it. I know an American expat who searched in vain for cocoa powder in the supermarkets here as she thought of it as a baking product, whereas in Denmark you would find it in the drinks aisle. I can be pretty fearless when it comes to finding food (as the anecdote above shows!), and I will also get hold of a shop assistant and ask them where to find the product. We all can recognise everyday food but the variation in types of milk, for example, can leave you stumped.

I have also found that often the picture on the front of a pack will be a serving suggestion, not a reflection of the content. Again, another expat shared a story where she struggled to find brown sugar. She saw a box with a picture of a well-known Danish coconut cake on the front and assumed the contents were coconut based and not sugar based. After she told me that story, I noticed that this was often the case and can easily lead to confusion.

We were lucky enough to have a supermarket visit as part of our relocation package. At the time I thought, 'How hard can it be?' but I found it really useful and very much missed having this when we moved to Germany. I recall walking around our new Berlin neighbourhood in the dark and rain searching in vain for the large local supermarket I could see on Google Maps but which appeared elusive in the real life. Once I did find it I was rather underwhelmed by the selection, and it took me a long time to find places to buy even my normal, simple foodstuffs.

OPENING HOURS

Both the UK and the USA are very consumer (and consumption) driven societies, but a lot of Europe is still catching up with that. In France shops shut for a long period in the middle of the day but stay open later. Strangely, I once saw a sandwich shop in a small town in France closed for the lunch period, when surely they would have done the most business. They also have early closing one day a week in some towns, even pretty big ones.

Many countries such as Denmark and Germany still observe Sunday as a day when the majority of shops close, and during the week most shops will close by 6pm at the latest. It can take some getting used to, especially if you are used to a 24-hour superstore close to your home, but you soon adjust to this. As I mentioned previously, be aware of the new public holidays in your new country as these are likely to be different to what you are used to and will have an impact on shop opening times.

SEASONS

There is also more of an emphasis on seasonal produce in many European countries, which can seem restrictive in the start when half your favourite recipes are not possible exactly when you want to make them. The plus point to this is that you are eating the produce at its prime and not force grown or shipped unripe. There is also less emphasis on using a lot of preservatives in food. There is sometimes a perception that food 'goes off' quickly, but it could be seen as the reverse: that foods with a lot of preservatives last an artificially long time. There is also less (if any) vitamin or mineral fortification added to foods in many European countries.

Another thing is to buy seasonal clothes and things when you see them as they will not necessarily be restocked. I have found this to be true in France, Denmark and Germany. As soon as winter boots and clothes are available, buy them, as they will sell out quickly. The same goes for anything advertised as special offers.

CLOTHING SIZES

Even if there are clothing stores you are familiar with such as H&M, there will be differences. Sizing, for example, may vary. In Denmark, on average women are taller than in the UK and you will find trouser lengths will reflect this. Likewise, men's clothes will often be cut according to the local physique, so again Danish men are tall but generally more slender than their British counterparts and this is reflected in the sizing. At the start you will also need to have a size comparison chart saved on your phone for clothing and shoes sizes (especially children's) to understand a different size system.

MEDICATION, GLASSES AND TEETH

The across-the-counter medications in different countries will vary both in choice and also by what is considered suitable for sale without a prescription. I would advise people moving to a new country to get a supply of your everyday medications before you move to ensure you are not worrying about finding them when you really need them. For example, allergy relief, painkillers, flu and cold remedies, children's medication (especially as for very young children and babies many European pharmacies will only sell suppositories) and eczema creams – whatever you use through the year. Also, go to your doctor before you leave and ask to have any prescription medicines filled before you leave so again you are not rushing to the doctors straight away. My UK GP gave me a prescription for a year's worth of the Pill before I left.

Once you do need to get medicines in your new country keep hold of your original packaging and find out the generic name of the drug rather than the brand name, as the pharmacist can use this to look up the local equivalent.

If you wear glasses have an eye test before you leave so you don't have to worry about this in the first year, and the same goes for a dental check up.

this is it – six months and onwards

About six months into your relocation is the time when reality really hits. For some this can be a challenging time and for others a time when you start to feel at home.

DON'T VISIT 'HOME' TOO SOON

I believe that it is often a mistake to go back 'home' for a visit within the first six months as this can remind you more about what you are missing and also can be a hinderance to settling in. When I was choosing where to go to university I decided against the one closest to my home, even though they were offering me a very good deal, as I feared that at the first hurdle I would run home for a home cooked meal and some parental love. I wanted to be able to deal with things myself, as in the long-run the option to always go home when things were difficult wouldn't be there. I think the same is true of relocation. If this is now your home, you need to tackle that and make it work, you can't be going 'home' every time you feel miserable. A much better option is to have people come and visit you, but not too soon. Show off your new home and city. Talking to them about the challenges and lows without a direct comparison hitting you in the face helps put it into perspective.

Once you feel more settled a visit back to your home country then is fun and not an escape. Going back to your home country after some time away often shows you both what you love about it, but also highlights the plus points of your new home.

SPEND THE HOLIDAYS EXPLORING

I know many expats who, as soon as the school holidays are upon them, pack up their families and disappear back to their home countries for the whole summer. I am not saying that you shouldn't use some of the long summer break to visit friends and families, but it is also the perfect time to enjoy your new country and do some exploring. Set out a list of day trips to do in the city and close by, and explore places that during work and term time you don't have time to visit.

Book a longer spell somewhere that the local people would go to. If you are in Germany many people head to the Baltic coast for a summer break, so why not try this out? Likewise, there will be other historic parts of your new country that you could reach and explore easily by train. It all helps you get more of a connection with the history, culture and geography of your new country.

Another reason to stick around if you have kids is to help them more with integrating with other children and the culture. In many cities museums organise holiday activities and there are holiday clubs centred around specific interests. The message you can give by always leaving your new country in the holidays to return 'home' is that this isn't somewhere to put down roots and that it is only temporary.

THIS IS 'IT'

Once you have hit the six months mark a feeling of permanence can start to set in. In the early stages everything is still new and you are finding your feet, but from about six months on you start to feel that this is 'it'.

'It' can be positive – you know your way around the city, you have mastered grocery shopping, you are starting to understand some of the language and you and your family are beginning to make friends and lay down roots. You can begin to relax a little and start to enjoy life more. If you fall into this category, that is great.

'It' can also be negative – you still don't feel you have made any friends, the language is still a mystery and there are everyday aspects to life that always get you down and that you can't see how to change. You mention this to friends from home whose response is, 'Well, you chose to do it'. This is the point when you have to go back to the mantra of being kind to yourself. You can't always expect to feel settled straight away but there are ways to start to tackle this, and they work at this time as much as at the beginning. Settling into a new city and country is not always quick, nor easy. There is also no shame in admitting that perhaps your new life isn't working for you and returning home.

Whilst much of this book aims to help you in the first six months of relocating somewhere new, there is still a lot to be gained by re-reading sections after you have been settled for six months to a year. The concept of being kind to yourself is the biggest lesson that I hope you have taken away from this book. No matter how others find relocation your experience is always unique to you, and every time you relocate it will be different. By equipping yourself with practical help and advice you are part of the way there, but the most important element of a successful relocation is dealing effectively with your feelings and emotions and those of your family.

I hope that what I have shared in the previous sixteen chapters will go some way towards helping you having a successful and positive relocation experience, and that you feel you can dip back into the book when you need more support.

I wish you all the very best with your relocation experience.

about the author

Melanie Haynes is a relocation consultant, blogger and writer based in Copenhagen, where she has lived for the last nine year excluding a character building eighteen months in Berlin. Through her consultancy she helps people planning to move to Copenhagen or already living there to have a positive relocation experience. She regularly writes about expat life in Denmark in The Local Denmark and the Huffington Post as well as on her popular blog, Dejlige Days. She has also appeared in various media including the Guardian and The Sunday Times and also in the Danish media talking about life as a seasoned expat in the Danish capital.

Dejlige Days: My Guide to a Successful Relocation is her first book and is like a friend sharing her best advice about relocation through her own personal experience of both good and bad relocation.

She lives with her husband and son close to the beach in Copenhagen.

www.ingramcontent.com/pod-product-compliance
Lightning Source LLC
Chambersburg PA
CBHW070841310526
45793CB00010B/310